Earth Keepers

MARJORY STONEMAN DOUGLAS

Voice of the Everglades

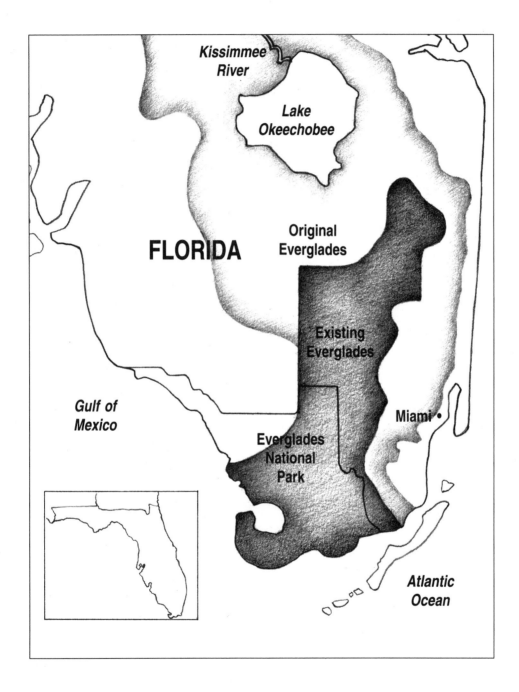

Kissimmee
River

Lake
Okeechobee

FLORIDA

Original
Everglades

Existing
Everglades

Gulf of
Mexico

Miami •

Everglades
National
Park

Atlantic
Ocean

Earth   *Keepers*

MARJORY STONEMAN DOUGLAS

Voice of the Everglades

Jennifer Bryant
Illustrated by Larry Raymond

Twenty-First Century Books

A Division of Henry Holt and Co., Inc.

Frederick, Maryland

Published by
Twenty-First Century Books
A Division of Henry Holt and Co., Inc.
38 South Market Street
Frederick, Maryland 21701

Printed in Mexico

10 9 8 7 6 5 4 3 2 1

Library of Congress Cataloging in Publication Data

Bryant, Jennifer
Marjory Stoneman Douglas: Voice of the Everglades
Illustrated by Larry Raymond

(An Earth Keepers Book)
Includes glossary and index.
Summary: Traces the life of the woman who became known
as the "Grandmother of the Glades" for her fight to preserve
the Florida Everglades against misuse and development.
1. Douglas, Marjory Stoneman—Juvenile literature.
2. Conservationists—Florida—Biography—Juvenile literature.
3. Everglades (Fla.)—Juvenile literature.
[1. Douglas, Marjory Stoneman. 2. Conservationists. 3. Everglades (Fla.)]
I. Raymond, Larry, ill. II. Title.
III. Series: Earth Keepers
QH31.D645B79   1992
333.7′2′092—dc20 [B] 91-39874 CIP AC
ISBN 0-8050-2113-2

Contents

Chapter 1

A Tough Old Woman

It was a typical summer night for southern Florida: hot and muggy. The air was so heavy that it was hard to breathe. It was the kind of night that made people restless and kept mosquitoes busy.

But it was hardly a typical night for the people who crowded into a Miami school auditorium. Most of them had left the comfort of their air-conditioned homes to come to this meeting of the Dade County planning department. They had come because they were angry.

Many of these people owned land in an area known as the East Everglades. They wanted to build homes and businesses there. But the members of the planning board had recommended against draining this swampy area. If the marshy acres of the East Everglades were not drained, the people who owned land there would not be able to build. On this night, the members of the planning board had to make a final decision.

A thousand landowners attended this public meeting. The heat didn't help anyone's mood. Speaker after speaker demanded that the board approve the draining. To them, the "Glades" was just a swamp, a breeding ground for mosquitoes—a nuisance, and no more. Why not reclaim this land, they argued, and make it useful?

Also attending the meeting was a small, 91-year-old woman named Marjory Stoneman Douglas. Her face was framed by thick glasses, almost covered by a huge, floppy hat. She had to be helped to the speaker's platform.

Heads turned as she walked slowly toward the front of the room. Was this the woman, people whispered, they had heard so much about? Was this little old lady the one they called the "Grandmother of the Glades"?

"Go home, Granny!" shouted one angry landowner.

"Mind your own business!" someone else yelled.

The angry crowd didn't bother Douglas. She had faced such meetings before. For more than 60 years, she had been hearing these kinds of arguments. Marjory Douglas was used to fighting back. Douglas's eyesight had gotten weaker with age, but her voice was as strong as ever. "I can't see you back there," she said, "but if you're standing up, you might as well sit down. I've got all night, and I'm used to the heat."

9

Her clear and confident voice took the noisy crowd by surprise. When the room was quiet, Marjory explained that this "swamp" was a vital part of a unique ecosystem, a natural network of living things and their environment. She described the Glades as a thousands-year-old balance of land and water, of sun and rain, of people and wildlife. This "swamp," she said, was a vast and beautiful system formed by these natural relationships.

The East Everglades, Douglas observed, was only one part of an ecosystem that stretches for over 9,000 square miles of central and southern Florida. Douglas described how storm clouds from the Gulf of Mexico drift over the Florida peninsula with their store of precious rain. The rainwater runs from the lakes of central Florida to the Kissimmee River, which used to wander for a hundred miles through a wetland home for fish and waterfowl.

The Kissimmee empties into huge Lake Okeechobee (the Indian name for "Big Water"). From there, the water spills out in a vast sheet of wetland, a slow and massive flow of water that inches its way down the peninsula to the Gulf of Mexico. These south Florida marshlands, with their endless stretches of thick, tough sedge called saw grass, make up the 4,000-square-mile area known as the Everglades. Here, beneath the hot Florida sun, the water evaporates and forms the drifting rain clouds that start the watery cycle once again.

It was Marjory Douglas who first realized that this vast sheet of water, moving too slowly for the eye to see and often less than a foot deep, was not a swamp but, in fact, a river. "A river of grass," she called the Glades, just as the native tribes of south Florida had called this area Pahayokee, or "Grassy Water." In her book, *The Everglades:*

River of Grass, first published in 1948, she described this mysterious world of water and grass, a world so simple and enduring that it holds "the secrets of time."

It was Douglas who first observed that the Everglades is part of a much larger ecosystem, a network of "water, weather, and wildlife." And she saw that this network, despite its vast reach, is a fragile and easily endangered one. She knew that disrupting any part of this natural network would damage the whole system. To block the flow of water with dams and drains would threaten the very life of the natural ecosystem.

"With less water in the Kissimmee River, there is less water for Lake Okeechobee," she noted, "and less water to flow to the Everglades, and less water to evaporate into rainfall to feed the river once again." Douglas painted a picture of a system similar to the human body's circulatory system. "If the flow stops," she insisted, "it would mean the destruction of south Florida."

And it is Marjory Douglas, this little old lady with the big, floppy hat, who has led the fight to preserve the Everglades against misuse and development. As founder and president of a group called Friends of the Everglades, Douglas has battled every effort to destroy this watery world. "I'm just a tough old woman," she says. But for

60 years, this tough, old woman has been the best friend of the Everglades.

Marjory Stoneman Douglas is a persuasive speaker. She likes to remind people that she took a course in elocution, or public speaking, as a college student. "I've been going around elocuting ever since," she says.

That muggy summer night, her "elocuting" was again successful. After Marjory's speech, the crowd remained silent. The members of the planning board, who now had to make the final decision, had heard both sides of the argument. When the vote was taken, Marjory Stoneman Douglas and her supporters—Marjory's Army, they were called—had carried the day. There would be no draining and no further development of the Everglades.

Marjory Douglas knew there would be other battles ahead. She knew that she would lose some of them. But she had won this one. And she was ready to go on with the fight.

*"I still don't believe everything
people tell me."*

Chapter 2

A Logical Child

Marjory Stoneman Douglas was born on April 7, 1890, in Minneapolis, Minnesota. Her father, she later wrote, was "six-feet-two and broad shouldered, the kind of man who got handsomer as he got older." Frank Stoneman's family traced its roots to the Quakers. "Of all the religious people that sought refuge in America, the Quakers were the most independent—and the most pigheaded," Marjory Douglas claims.

Douglas traces her own character to this Quaker spirit. "I feel both independent and pigheaded as well," she says.

Her ancestors, Marjory observes, "were a courageous and quick-thinking people. They read books constantly. They remembered what they read and made up their own minds concerning it." Her great-great uncle, Levi Coffin, was a leader of the Underground Railroad, the organization that helped slaves escape to freedom in the North.

"He was a great inspiration to me," Marjory wrote, "as a free-thinker and an activist."

Frank Stoneman seemed to inherit this independent, risk-taking temperament. As a young man, he went off to Billings, Montana, where he hoped to make his fortune. Marjory's father opened the first grocery store in Billings.

Frank Stoneman didn't bring back his fortune when he returned to Minneapolis. But he did bring back tales of the Montana frontier. Many years later, Marjory would remember her father's stories about playing checkers with a retired soldier named Beanbelly Brown.

Stoneman met Marjory's mother, Lillian Trefethen, on his return to Minneapolis. Her mother's family was part French and part British. Marjory's British ancestors were "seagoing people," she wrote. "Every sea in the world was known to the Trefethens."

But, according to Marjory, "all the French side of her family came out" in her mother. Lillian had "marvelous black hair" and eyes "like brown velvet." To Marjory, "she was particularly beautiful all her life."

Marjory's parents did not have much in common. Her mother certainly did not share the adventurous spirit of Frank Stoneman.

As Marjory Douglas later wrote, "There was a good deal of difference between their temperaments":

> "The Western people, my father's family, were more hardy. They adjusted easily to discomforts or handicaps and tried to do something about it. Where my mother was brought up, the way of life was pretty settled. Bad things didn't happen so much, and the people were more upset when they did."

For several years, this difference didn't seem to matter. Frank and Lillian Stoneman were married and moved into the first apartment house in Minneapolis, called Netley Corner. Marjory was their only child. "I see myself sitting on the stairs going down to the kitchen, being fed out of a pan of warm, creamed potatoes," she recalls. "It is my only memory of that time."

Her father's business failed when Marjory was three, and the Stonemans moved to Providence, Rhode Island. Her memories of this time are peaceful and happy ones. Lillian, a talented musician, often gave evening concerts for friends and neighbors on her Steinway piano. "My mother always began by saying that her little girl was upstairs and going to sleep," Marjory remembers. "Then she played the Brahms Lullaby."

Upstairs, Frank Stoneman would read to Marjory. The tale of Hiawatha was one of her early favorites. But there was one part of the story that caused Marjory "to burst into loud sobs":

> "I couldn't make him understand I was sorry for the birch tree, because why should the birch tree have to give up its bark just because Hiawatha wanted to build a canoe? I couldn't stand it. I cried, and I guess father skipped the canoe part after that."

Young Marjory loved *Alice in Wonderland*, too, but she "couldn't quite accept the idea of a rabbit with a waistcoat and a watch. I was a logical child," she explains, "and I'd never seen a rabbit like that. So I remained skeptical about the whole business."

When Marjory was four, she went with her parents on a trip to Florida. She would always remember "the marvelous light, the wonderful white tropic light."

Her father's business was again unsuccessful, and the family had to move, Marjory recalls, "somewhere on the outskirts of Providence." She can still picture the little lake nearby. "I saw sunlight on the waves of the lake and was excited and exhilarated by the brightness of the air, the sunshine, and the water."

Marjory and her mother liked to take evening walks together, "always arm in arm or holding hands." These walks, Marjory says, "were an important part of my closeness to my mother."

Although Marjory shared her father's inquisitive traits, she was closest to her mother. "I think I've never been so close to anyone," she observed. Almost a century later, Marjory recalls the quiet times when she would sit in her mother's lap, "and she would hold me and we would look out at the stars."

Marjory also remembers that this was the time when "terrible things" began to happen to her mother. The strain of Frank Stoneman's repeated business failures began to take a toll on Lillian's health.

Lillian could not adjust to what Marjory called "living on the edge" of things. Soon, her mother started to have "nervous spells" and, finally, a mental breakdown.

Soon after her mother's breakdown, Marjory's parents separated. Marjory was only six years old. "I was playing on the porch steps," Marjory wrote. "My mother appeared with a suitcase. She put my hat and jacket on me and announced: 'We're going to Taunton.' "

Marjory and her mother traveled to Taunton, a small town in Massachusetts, where they moved in with Lillian's parents and her sister, Marjory's Aunt Fanny. Years later, Marjory would remember how she often felt alone in her new home. "In the great family crisis, I was left to myself," Marjory said.

It was a stressful time for Marjory. "I remember going home," she recalls, "almost praying that nothing bad had happened that day, never knowing what the atmosphere of the house was going to be like."

For "a good many years," she said, "there were bad dreams, from which often I woke myself, screaming."

Marjory found that reading was a way to escape her troubled household. She didn't care to play with dolls, preferring instead to go off by herself to read one of her books. She began to write stories of her own and even invented a word puzzle that was published in *St. Nicholas*, a popular children's magazine.

Marjory was enrolled in the Barnam Street Elementary School. Reading and writing continued to be her strengths. Math was her weakest subject, especially when it came to fractions. Miss Francis, her teacher, tried to explain fractions by cutting up an apple. But even that didn't work. "I've always hated apples as well as fractions," Marjory pointed out years later.

Lillian Stoneman's mental state did not improve. For a brief period, she even had to go to a mental hospital. The Trefethens blamed Frank Stoneman for Lillian's illness and felt bitter toward him. Marjory had to decide for herself what she believed:

> *"I suppose the dislocation of my life, being the child of a broken family, made me somewhat of a skeptic and a dissenter. To this day, I still don't believe everything people tell me. In 1896, I particularly didn't believe things that were said in bitterness about my father."*

The companionship of her close girlfriends made up for some of the unhappiness in Marjory's family. But her relationships with boys didn't go nearly as well. Marjory never felt that boys found her attractive. She said that she was "the most disgusting looking baby you could possibly imagine" and grew up to be "a fat little child and a fat little girl." In high school, Marjory experienced "the awful ordeal of being a wallflower" at parties and dances. "I was fat, my hair was greasy, I wore glasses, I giggled, I was completely self-conscious with boys," she says.

As her senior year drew to a close, Marjory had to decide about attending college. She felt guilty about leaving her mother behind. "Her whole life had been centered around me," Marjory wrote, "and without me in the house she had nothing left to live for."

Fortunately, Grandmother Trefethen encouraged Marjory to begin a life of her own. "My grandmother saw very clearly what had to be done," Marjory says. "She understood that even if my mother's life depended on my staying at home, my life depended on getting away."

In the fall of 1908, Marjory left her Taunton home to attend Wellesley College, a women's college near Boston. It was only an hour and a half away by train. But as she was soon to discover, Marjory was beginning the journey of a lifetime.

*"You have to stand up for
some things in this world."*

Chapter 3

─────────────────────────────

A New Life

Marjory's grandmother was right. Marjory enjoyed "a great feeling of freedom" at Wellesley. "There was a new joy in life, in living, and in experience," she wrote.

For Marjory, college life brought a renewed delight in reading and writing. On her first day at Wellesley, she sat up by the light of an oil lamp and read, as she later recalled, "until late in the night." The first thing she had to do in English class was write a letter home. Marjory wrote about the beauty of the Wellesley campus. She read her letter to an appreciative class:

> *"That fall at Wellesley, the oak leaves were brilliant scarlet, and the scarlet was mirrored in the lake. The lake was blue and the sky was beautiful, and I talked about it in the letter. I got a big round of applause from the class and at once was established as a writer. That reputation stayed with me the rest of my days."*

Marjory also took an interest in public speaking. Her class in "expression" was taught by Malvina Bennett. As Marjory said, Bennett's "mission in life was to smooth off the edges of the various dialects and accents of students from all over the country."

Marjory recalls the exercises "we recited up and down the alphabet." For the b's, each student had to practice saying, "Balmy breezes bore my bark beneath balconies and bridges while Bill the boatman bumped the barge against the breastwork of the breakwater."

It wasn't enough just to get these tongue twisters right. Marjory and her classmates had to "throw our voices out, holler so loud we hit the back of the auditorium. Then we had to be whispery and still be heard across the room."

Wellesley also meant a different kind of freedom— freedom from boys. "A woman's college was the answer," Marjory wrote. "It freed me of the pressure of the boys' presence, which made me feel very self-conscious. Since I was still unattractive to them, at least at Wellesley they weren't around to remind me of it. I could forget all that. I could be myself as an individual."

For Marjory, part of being herself meant spending time with her many female friends. Throughout her years at Wellesley, Marjory made strong and lasting friendships.

She shared a working dormitory with seven other women. (In a working dormitory, the students do chores to help pay their college costs.) Marjory later wrote that her roommate, Carolyn Percy, was "a great force" in her life. It was a friendship that would last the rest of Marjory's life. "She understood me better than anyone else ever has," Marjory wrote.

"As Wellesley developed our skills," Marjory recalls, "we became more convinced of a woman's right to use them." In 1911, during her third year at Wellesley, Marjory and some of her friends formed a club to support the voting rights of women. (Until 1920, only men could vote.) "I was always for it," said Marjory. "You have to stand up for some things in this world."

Also during her junior year, Marjory discovered that her mother had cancer. An operation was needed, and Marjory remembers how she was with her mother "every minute in the hospital." The night before the operation, Marjory wrote, "my mother got into bed with me, and I held her in my arms all night."

As Marjory and her friends approached the end of their time at Wellesley, their thoughts turned toward the future. "Most of my friends knew exactly where they were going after college," she remembers. But as graduation day neared, Marjory found herself with the same feelings that she had before she entered college. She wanted to be on her own, but she felt that she should return home to take care of her mother.

On a beautiful summer day in June of 1912, Marjory and her friends paraded proudly in front of their families to receive their diplomas.

The day began as one of the happiest in Marjory's life, but it ended quite differently. After the graduation ceremonies were over, Aunt Fanny gave Marjory the bad news: Lillian was dying of cancer. Grief-stricken, Marjory rushed home.

Her mother was going through "frightful pain," Marjory remembers. "It was terrible to see her suffer." Only a few weeks later, Lillian Stoneman died.

After her mother's death, Marjory said that she was "completely lonely" and confused about what she should do. She took a job in a department store, but she felt "like a misfit." Years later, Marjory described herself at this time as living "on the edge of things. It wasn't life, it was just making a living." Marjory had no sense of direction and, she recalls, "no power of judgment over anything."

Her lack of judgment was clear when Marjory married a man named Kenneth Douglas. Marjory admitted that "it wasn't love" that led her to marry this man. In fact, she later wrote, "I couldn't have told you anything about him." But, for Marjory, it was at least a change.

It was also a mistake. Marjory soon discovered that her husband was involved in illegal business activities. In a few months, Kenneth Douglas was in jail, and Marjory became convinced that their marriage would never work.

A surprise visit from her father's brother, Dr. Edward Stoneman, came at just the right moment. "Your father has recently married again," Marjory's Uncle Ned told her. "I am anxious that you leave your husband and go down to Florida. It's time you knew your father—you've been separated a very long time."

With nothing to lose, Marjory packed her bags and headed south. It was September 1915. Marjory Stoneman Douglas was 25 years old, and, once again, she was starting a new life:

> *"I left my marriage and all my past history without a single regret. I was heading south with a sense of release, excitement, and anticipation. I was seeing my father again for the first time since I was six years old."*

"I found what I was meant to do."

Chapter 4

A Great Step Forward

As the train pulled into the Miami station, Marjory Douglas worried that she wouldn't recognize her father. After all, she observed, she "had only the distant memories of a six-year-old." But Frank Stoneman found his daughter first. Marjory Douglas recalled the moment years later:

> " 'Hello, Sweetheart,' he said, and I said, 'Hello, Father,' and he kissed me—and there we were reunited with no fuss and feathers."

They drove to her father's house on the edge of town, past "a strange landscape that surrounded my new home." Her father's home was "a plain, little house," with open rooms and a large front porch. Waiting on the porch for Marjory was Frank's second wife, Lilla. Marjory Douglas remembers how her new stepmother "came dashing out" to greet her "with arms outspread," as if she had known her stepdaughter forever.

Later that evening, Marjory Stoneman Douglas and her father talked about the past. "He caught me up on his own life," she recalls.

Frank Stoneman had come to Orlando, Florida, in 1896 to set up a law practice. In 1906, he moved to Miami, where he started a newspaper, the *Miami News Record*, renamed the *Herald* in 1910. Marjory Douglas wrote that her father "was happy being the editor of a newspaper in a frontier community. He said he'd never lived in a finished town in his life."

It wasn't long before Douglas was working for the *Herald* as a reporter. At last, she had found a way to make use of her writing abilities. "It was as if everything that I had been doing since college had been all wrong," she later wrote. "Suddenly, I found what I was meant to do. I didn't care what I was writing about as long as it was writing. It was a great step forward."

Douglas wrote hundreds of articles about the people, places, and events that were shaping Florida during the early 1900s. At this time, south Florida was still a largely undeveloped area. With only 5,000 residents, Miami was little more than a railroad terminal. The people who came to live there shared the adventurous spirit that was so much a part of Douglas's own roots.

Douglas found the Florida landscape as untamed as the men and women who lived there. This was especially true for the area known as the Everglades. Douglas and her friends used to get up before daybreak to visit the Glades. They would build a fire and watch the sun rise. The sight would be hard for Douglas to forget: "There were the Everglades beyond us, completely untouched. The grass and the islands stood alone in the light and the beautiful air."

Great swoops of birds, as many as 40,000, surprised these early morning onlookers. White ibis, herons, egrets, eagles—birds were everywhere, and Marjory Douglas was a most enthusiastic observer:

> *"You could stand on the old roadway and look back toward a little bridge and see white ibis and wood stork sitting on the railings. You could walk over very quietly and watch the heron fishing. Owls in the trees would ask: 'Who cooks for yooo?' Way off in the distance, others would answer: 'I cooks for myself.'"*

Douglas was quickly drawn into the debate over the future of the Everglades. Many people, including Florida's governor, Napoleon Bonaparte Broward, were in favor of draining the Everglades. The land could then be used for development—for farms, homes, and roads. But others, like Frank Stoneman, disagreed. "Father had very strong opinions about draining the Everglades even then," said Douglas. Frank Stoneman supported the preservation of the Glades, an idea that made the developers furious. He wanted this wilderness area to be left untouched.

"My earliest notions about the Everglades," Douglas would later write, "came directly" from her father. She became convinced that the Glades should be preserved in a natural state. She joined a committee to establish the area as a national park, which would give the Everglades the protection of the federal government.

Douglas's life was now more settled than ever before. But with each passing day, she became more restless. The constant pressure of newspaper work, with its schedules and tight deadlines, left her tired and nervous. "I hadn't liked regular hours. I hadn't liked being told what to do, or working for other people," she wrote. "In a way I was a loner at work, the same way I was a loner at home. I wanted to be an individual."

In 1924, Douglas left the *Herald*. She had decided to devote her time to writing stories for popular magazines, like *The Saturday Evening Post* and *Ladies Home Journal*. Her stories often took place in and around the Everglades. One story told about the death of a man who tries to protect his land from poachers. (A poacher is a person who kills animals illegally.) Another story was about a boy and an old man who brave the dangerous journey across the Everglades.

Douglas liked her independence. In 1926, she moved into a house of her own in Coconut Grove, just outside of Miami. It was a simple home—she described it as one big room—but it was enough for her. "I didn't need much of a house, just a workshop, a place of my own. I hoped my little house would be as stout and sparse as a factory, with not much to worry about."

For the next 15 years, the money she made from writing stories enabled Marjory Douglas to support herself. The independent life didn't mean that Douglas didn't see her family. Several times a week, she would visit her father for an evening of checkers. Her Massachusetts family kept in touch, too. In 1938, Douglas journeyed to Taunton to see Aunt Fanny, who was dying. She was glad, she said, to hold her aunt's hand at the end.

Douglas also held her father's hand when he died later that year. Frank Stoneman was 84 years old and, according to Douglas, a tired man. She remarked that her father had decided "not to carry on." Douglas stayed with him as the doctors tried to operate to treat a kidney problem. "He said, 'You'll come with me?' and I said, 'Yes, Father, I'll be with you.' That was it."

Now truly on her own, Marjory Douglas continued to support herself by writing stories. In 1942, an editor and writer named Hervey Allen dropped by her house. Allen was working on a series of books called "The Rivers of America," and he asked Douglas to write a book about the Miami River.

"You can't write about the Miami River," she laughed. "It's only about an inch long." She asked him if she could write about the Everglades instead. After all, she reasoned, the Everglades was connected to the Miami River. Maybe she could get a book out of that. "All right," said Allen, "write about the Everglades."

"There, on a writer's whim and an editor's decision," Marjory Douglas recalled years later, "I was hooked with the idea that would consume me for the rest of my life."

She turned at once to Garald Parker, the Florida state hydrologist (a scientist who studies water). "What are the

Everglades?" Douglas asked him. Parker explained that the Everglades wasn't a swamp at all, but flowing water. "Wherever fresh water runs and the saw grass starts up," he said, "that's where you have the Everglades."

Marjory Douglas then asked Parker whether or not the Everglades could be called a river. He replied that "a river is a body of fresh water moving more in one direction than the other." Parker gave Douglas a map of the Glades to take home. She studied the map carefully, sitting and staring at the spread of water curving down from Lake Okeechobee toward the Ten Thousand Islands.

The more Marjory Douglas studied the map, the more she thought about Parker's simple description of a river. "If it's running water, and if there are ridges on either side," she thought, "maybe the ridges are an east bank and a west bank, and . . . maybe this really is a river."

"Do you think I could call it a river of grass?" an excited Douglas asked Parker. He agreed that it would be a good name.

According to Marjory Stoneman Douglas, those three words—river of grass—"changed everybody's knowledge as to what the Everglades meant."

Chapter 5

The River of Grass

"There are no other Everglades in the world."

With this simple sentence, Marjory Stoneman Douglas began her book on a place she described as "one of the unique regions of the earth." For hundreds of years, she wrote, the Glades was so mysterious that "they seemed more like a fantasy than a geographic and historic fact." The Everglades was the stuff of old stories and legends, considered by many people to be a poisonous marshland, a swampy home to pirates and outlaws, a place of evil.

The Everglades, as Douglas discovered, *is* a place of mystery, but it was the remarkable mysteries of nature that she wrote about. No place anywhere on the earth, Douglas reported, is like the Everglades:

"They are unique in the simplicity, the diversity, the related harmony of the forms of life that they enclose. The miracle of light pours over the green and brown expanse of saw grass and of water, shining and slowly moving, the grass and water that is the meaning and the central fact of the Everglades. It is a river of grass."

The "Grassy Water" of the Glades actually begins in central Florida at Lake Okeechobee. It is a huge, shallow dish of water. "A boat can push for hours in a day of white sun through the short, crisp lake waves," Douglas wrote, "and there will be nothing to be seen anywhere but the brightness where the color of the water and the color of the sky become one." She described how an eagle, "questing in great solitary circles," can look down all day long at the faintly green water—"and be seen and heard by no one at all."

At the southern edge of the great lake, where the water slops and seeps over rock and soil, the great mass of saw grass begins. "Where the grass and water are," Douglas pointed out, "there is the heart, the current, the meaning of the Everglades."

This "enormous curving river of grass" stretches from Lake Okeechobee to the Gulf of Mexico. The tough, dense saw grass is everywhere. To try to get through this vast, green world "is to be cut off from all air, to be beaten down by the sun and ripped by the grassy, saw-toothed edges as one sinks in mud and water." The water flows from Lake Okeechobee down the rivers of central Florida.

The only source of water is rain. "Here the rain is everything," Douglas observed. The rains begin in late spring. An April chill surprises "the stuffy, wet heat and brassy sunlight." Off in the distance, there is a great piling up of clouds and the heavy, bumping sound of thunder. The winds begin to change. Then the rain sends down "a long, slashing burst in which even hailstones may bounce like popcorn against the darkening land."

The full force of the rains, however, is not felt until late summer, when the massive gulf clouds march across the landscape. Rose-colored by the summer sunset, these mountainous shapes send smashing sheets of rain against the earth—as much as 10 or 12 inches in a single day.

Thousands of acres of saw grass, Douglas observed, "burst into a million million flashes from as many gleaming and trembling drops of wet, flashing back their red and emerald and diamond lights."

The waters rise and begin their southward flow:

> *"The Kissimmee River is swollen and strongly swirling between its wet, marshy banks, but still the water does not move off fast enough. The banks are overflowing, and the spongy ground between it and Fisheating Creek is all one swamp. The rains fling their solid shafts of water down the streaming green land, and Okeechobee swells and stirs and creeps south down the unseen tilt of the Glades."*

The floods are vital to the health of the Everglades ecosystem, nourishing the rich soil and providing wildlife with secure habitats.

Without the flood waters of the Florida summer, there would be no Everglades.

In the dry season, Douglas wrote, "the water shrinks below the grass roots." The yellow sun of winter dries up the early morning dew, strung like a cobweb of pearls. The ground dries and cracks. In the hardened earth, one can see the pattern of sharp toes and a heavy, dragging belly, where "some alligator has hitched his slow armored length from one drying water hole to another." Schools of fish, revealed by the receding waters, attract egrets, herons, spoonbills, wood storks, and bald eagles.

This is the round of the seasons, a cycle of dry and wet months as evenly balanced as a set of scales. The balance of sun and rain keeps secure a world of natural diversity. The Glades are home to what Douglas called a "crowd of changing forms, of thrusting, teeming life."

There is the "strange jungle" of plants, from the yellow catkin to the custard apple tree, from the "green curtains" of the mysterious moonvines to the pine forests of the Glades' eastern border.

There is the endless assortment of birds, fish, and insects. There are the deer and wildcats, the alligators and rattlesnakes. Here, the elusive panther prowls the open spaces of the cypress groves, the stout-hearted black bear digs for tasty crabs and turtle eggs, the barred owl hoots far off in the night, and the playful mother otter makes a mud slide for her cubs.

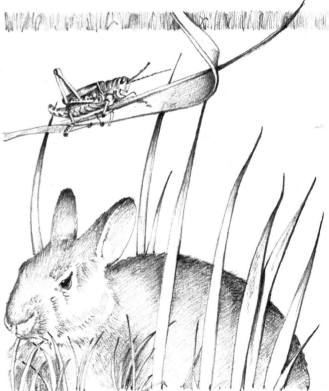

For tens of thousands of years, the Everglades were a world where these forms of life lived in what Douglas described as "a finely balanced harmony." But Douglas's book also detailed how endangered this harmony was.

Florida became a state in 1845, and "almost at once," Douglas wrote, people began to promote the idea of draining the Everglades. In 1848, a government report said that draining the Glades would be easy. There would be "no bad effects," the report concluded.

Despite the failure of some early drainage attempts, the project received the support of state officials. A building boom encouraged thousands of people from across the country to own a piece of the Everglades. Canals and dams were dug to prevent or control seasonal flooding. Farmers grew vegetables in the rich muck of the south Florida marshland. Ranchers fattened their cattle on dry land throughout the winter months. New railway lines sprung up to connect the communities of settlers who had come to Florida to seek their fortunes.

But the ecosystem of the Everglades was not suited for either farming or ranching. The natural cycle of dry and wet seasons brought a devastating series of droughts and floods. The weather proved to be a bitter enemy to Florida homesteaders.

In 1926 and again in 1928, south Florida was struck by hurricanes. The hurricane of September 17, 1926, was described by Douglas as a "screaming, blowing terror." Nobody even knew how strong the storm was, Douglas noted, because the weather instruments set up to measure the winds were blown away. The hurricane took the lives of 320 people and drowned the hopes of thousands of farmers and ranchers.

The 1928 hurricane was even worse, taking more than 1,800 lives. "A long, howling wind swept the lake waters over the cleared lands, over the canals, the cane fields, the scattered houses, the far roads," wrote Douglas. "Lives were smashed out under tons of water in the night. Dawn disclosed a wilderness of water."

Floods and droughts had always been a part of the south Florida environment. But now that the land had been drained and developed for farms and homes, people demanded protection from the natural cycle of wet and dry seasons that kept the Everglades ecosystem secure.

A huge dam was built to hold back the flood waters of Lake Okeechobee. A concrete network of canals was designed to bring water from the lake area to surrounding farmland in the dry season. The sound of dynamite was heard across the Glades.

"Business boomed in the lake towns," Douglas wrote. "The landscape became crammed with the bustle of people making money in a hurry." More and more acres of the watery grass were cleared for farms, ranches, and housing.

More and more trucks and railway cars shipped more and more produce to eager customers across the country, from Massachusetts to California. And more and more, with each passing day, the Everglades were dying.

"Where there had been the flow of the river of grass," Douglas said, "there were only brackish, drying pools and mosquitoes. The saw grass died, rustling like paper."

Douglas noted how fires roared uncontrolled through the dry grass. "The whole Everglades were burning," she wrote. "What had once been a river of grass and sweet water had now become a river of fire."

At last, there was a public outcry for change. "Now that it was almost too late," wrote Douglas, "men began to realize that the water supply was never just a local problem, to be settled in makeshift bits and pieces. The Everglades were one vast unified harmonious whole in which the old subtle balance, which had been destroyed, must somehow be replaced." A new, scientific study of the region recommended that the lower area of the Glades become a national park.

Marjory Douglas had campaigned for almost 20 years to convince the government to establish such a park. In 1947, the Everglades National Park was formally opened by President Harry Truman. Although the boundaries of the park covered only a fraction of the Everglades ecosystem, most environmentalists were pleased to see at least a portion of the region protected.

Douglas attended the opening ceremonies. The park, she said, was "a great accomplishment."

That same year, Douglas's book, *The Everglades: River of Grass*, was published. The book was quite successful and brought popular attention to the plight of the Glades. It seemed that the struggle to save the environment of the region was finally being won.

Marjory Douglas concluded her book on a hopeful note. She wrote:

> *"Perhaps even in this last hour, in a new relationship of usefulness and beauty, the vast, magnificent, subtle and unique region of the Everglades may not be utterly lost."*

But it was not "the last hour" in this environmental struggle. In fact, although Douglas could not know it, the fight for the Everglades had just begun.

"It was almost as if the Everglades had waited for me."

Chapter 6
=========

Friend of the Glades

The publication of *The Everglades: River of Grass* was both an end and a beginning for Marjory Douglas. It was the end of five years of hard work. But it was just the beginning of Douglas's work as an environmental activist.

Despite the popularity of her book, government efforts to channel and dam the water supply of south Florida continued. "The danger is not over," Douglas warned.

In 1948, only one year after the Everglades National Park was established, the U.S. Army Corps of Engineers, according to one report, "built or improved 1,400 miles of canals and levees, complete with tide gates, floodgates, and pumps to suck water off the flooded farmland."

In the 1960s, the Army Corps decided to "improve" the Kissimmee River. It launched a mammoth effort to straighten out the meandering course of the river. The Kissimmee, which once wandered for a hundred miles through the marshland of the central Florida countryside, was turned into a 52-mile ditch. The flood land became farmland, and the great river of grass now moved through gates and dikes and pumps controlled by water managers.

The "improved" water supply system was a disaster for the Everglades. The water level of the park shrank. Waste products and pesticides from cattle ranches and farms polluted Okeechobee and surrounding waterways. Wildlife populations dwindled as homes and nesting areas were destroyed. Plans for further development, including a huge jetport to be built near the northern border of the park, threatened the future of the entire ecosystem.

The huge earth-moving machines that rolled into the Everglades were met by angry protesters. One of them was Joe Browder, who worked for the National Audubon Society. Browder came to Marjory Douglas for help. He asked her to speak out against the jetport.

Douglas was not sure what to do. "I suggested that such things are more effective if they come from organizations," she recalled saying to Browder. "Without skipping a beat, he said, 'Why don't you start an organization?' "

For Marjory Douglas, the time had come to take a stand. "The Everglades were always a topic, but now they promised to become more than that," she wrote. "They promised to become a reason for things, a central force in my existence."

Douglas was now 78 years old. She had always been a fighter, but now she found something that was really worth fighting for. "It was almost as if the Everglades had waited for me," Douglas said.

She knew, of course, that she could not do it alone. So Douglas followed Browder's suggestion and founded a group called Friends of the Everglades. It cost a dollar to join.

As president of the group, Marjory Douglas began a new career. She traveled throughout central and southern Florida, she said, "making speeches to every organization that would listen." She wrote that her "college elocution training from 60 years earlier came in handy here. I got 15 or 20 new members every time I spoke. In a year we had over 500, and in another year over 1,000, and later 3,000 members from 38 states."

The jetport was never finished. In 1970, under pressure from environmental groups, the state government agreed to locate the project elsewhere. Marjory's Army, as her group came to be known, had won a major battle.

But the "war" for south Florida was far from over. Throughout the 1970s and 1980s, Douglas continued to champion the cause of preserving the Everglades. Though her eyesight grew increasingly worse, she insisted on a busy schedule of speaking engagements. "No matter how poor my eyes are, I can still talk," she said confidently.

In 1975, Douglas was named Conservationist of the Year by the Florida Audubon Society. She was awarded the same honor by the Florida Wildlife Federation a year later. In 1989, she was made honorary vice president of the Sierra Club, a national environmental group.

For Marjory Stoneman Douglas, though, the public's concern about the threatened Everglades ecosystem was the best reward.

In the late 1970s, the South Florida Water Management Board decided to return the Kissimmee River to its original channel. The huge ditch built by the U.S. Army Corps of Engineers would be filled in, and the Kissimmee would once again wander across the central Florida landscape.

Hundreds of thousands of acres of land have been added to the Everglades National Park. Marshland that had been drained is being restored. Restrictions have been placed on land development and farming practices that pollute the water supply. Conservation programs are now under way to preserve the supply of fresh water.

In January of 1991, Lawton Chiles, the governor of Florida, stated his support for these efforts to save the Glades. "Floridians have spent most of the century trying to destroy the Everglades," he said. "I hope to see the day when we have restored as much of the Everglades as we can, when we have finally learned to live in peace with the Everglades, when we can simply allow it to be."

Only two months later, Governor Chiles signed a new law that was designed to clean up the Everglades. The official signing ceremony was held in Marjory Stoneman Douglas's front yard.

Chapter 7

The Legacy of the Glades

Today, they call Marjory Douglas the "Grandmother of the Glades." This very active "grandmother" continues to lead a campaign to preserve the ecosystem she first described, with great power and beauty, more than 40 years ago. Since she joined the Everglades park committee in the 1920s, she has seen the rapid ruin of that ecosystem and a slow return to balance.

Most encouraging to Marjory Douglas is the outlook for future generations. She is pleased to see the growth of environmental education programs for young people. "It's enormously important. The children are our whole future," Douglas believes.

The Marjory Stoneman Douglas Nature Center in Key Biscayne, Florida, is one of many places where children and adults alike can learn more about the natural world and what they can do to preserve the environment. To Marjory, the center is a symbol of hope. It represents a

change in the way people think about the natural world, an attitude of responsibility for our environment.

Now, when she sits on her front porch and wonders about the future of the Everglades, Marjory Douglas is more confident than ever that they will survive. "It would be the first time," she remarks, "that a region that has almost gone to complete ruin has been brought back by the understanding and wisdom of its citizens."

Douglas knows that, one day, her own life will end. But the thought of death doesn't scare her. "I think this life has been plenty," she says. "It's just about all anybody could take, really. I'm cheerful about the feeling the end will come—let it come."

But even when Marjory Stoneman Douglas is gone, her legacy—an unwavering dedication to preserving the "river of grass"—will live on.

Glossary

canal	a waterway dug across land
conservation	the process by which natural resources are saved, or conserved
dam	a wall built across a stream or river to hold back water
dike	an earthen dam
drain	to empty an area of water
drought	an extended period of time without rain
ecology	the study of living things in their environment
ecosystem	the network of relationships among living things and their environment
environment	the physical world that surrounds a plant or animal
environmentalist	a person who seeks to protect the natural environment
Everglades	a vast, shallow, slow-moving river in south Florida
flood	a great flow of water over dry land
floodgate	a gate used to control the flow of water

homesteader	a person who makes a home in a newly settled place
hurricane	a severe tropical storm with strong winds (exceeding 75 miles per hour) and heavy rains
hydrology	the scientific study of water
marsh	an area of low-lying, wet land; a swamp
pesticide	a substance, often a strong chemical, used to kill insect pests
poacher	a person who kills animals illegally
pollution	the process by which a natural environment is made unclean and unfit for living things
preservation	the process by which an environment is kept, or preserved, in its natural condition
restoration	the process by which a damaged environment is restored to its natural condition
river	a large stream of water that flows into an ocean, lake, or other body of water
saw grass	a type of grass or sedge with tough, sharp edges
swamp	a low-lying area often filled with water; a marsh
wildlife	animals or plants living in a natural state
wildlife refuge	an area of land or water set aside as a protected home for wildlife

Index

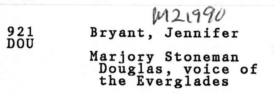

921
DOU

Bryant, Jennifer

Marjory Stoneman
Douglas, voice of
the Everglades

$14.95

DATE			